SCHOLASTIC
ENGLISH SKILLS

Grammar and punctuation
Workbook

Ages 5–7

Grammar and punctuation

Book End, Range Road, Witney, Oxfordshire, OX29 0YD
www.scholastic.co.uk

© 2015, Scholastic Ltd

8 9   8 9 0 1 2 3 4

British Library Cataloguing-in-Publication Data
A catalogue record for this book is available from the British Library.

ISBN 978-1407-14070-4
Printed by Replika Press Pvt. Ltd, India

Every effort has been made to trace copyright holders for the works reproduced in this book, and the publishers apologise for any inadvertent omissions.

Author
Lesley Fletcher

Editorial
Rachel Morgan, Jenny Wilcox, Red Door Media, Suzanne Adams

Design
Neil Salt and Nicolle Thomas

Cover Design
Nicolle Thomas

Illustration
Cathy Hughes

Cover Illustration
Eddie Rego

Contents

How to use this book

- *Scholastic English Skills Workbooks* help your child to practise and improve their skills in English.

- The content is divided into topics. Find out what your child is doing in school and dip into the practice activities as required.

- Keep the working time short and come back to an activity if your child finds it too difficult. Ask your child to note any areas of difficulty. Don't worry if your child does not 'get' a concept first time, as children learn at different rates and content is likely to be covered at different times throughout the school year.

- Check your child's answers at www.scholastic.co.uk/ses/grammar.

- Give lots of encouragement, complete the 'How did you do' for each activity and the progress chart as your child finishes each chapter.

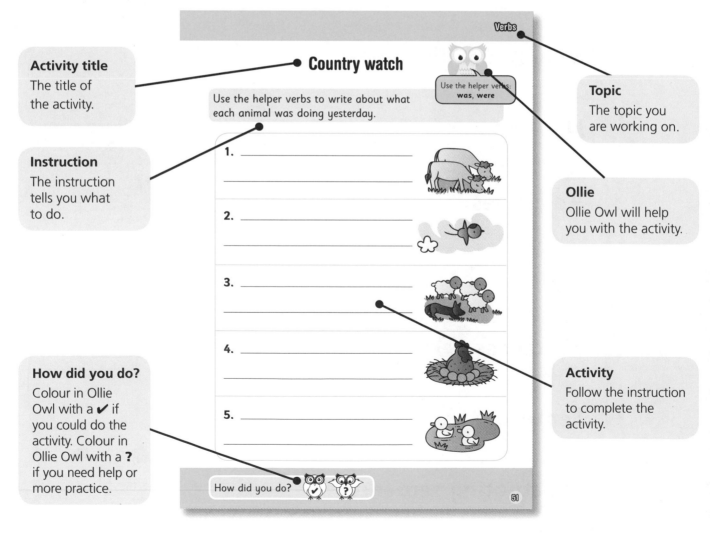

Activity title
The title of the activity.

Instruction
The instruction tells you what to do.

How did you do?
Colour in Ollie Owl with a ✔ if you could do the activity. Colour in Ollie Owl with a ? if you need help or more practice.

Topic
The topic you are working on.

Ollie
Ollie Owl will help you with the activity.

Activity
Follow the instruction to complete the activity.

If you need help, ask an adult!

Sort them out

Write these naming words in the correct box.

cat   orange   dog   woman   baby
carrot   girl   banana   lion   leek   potato
lemon   man   broccoli   rabbit

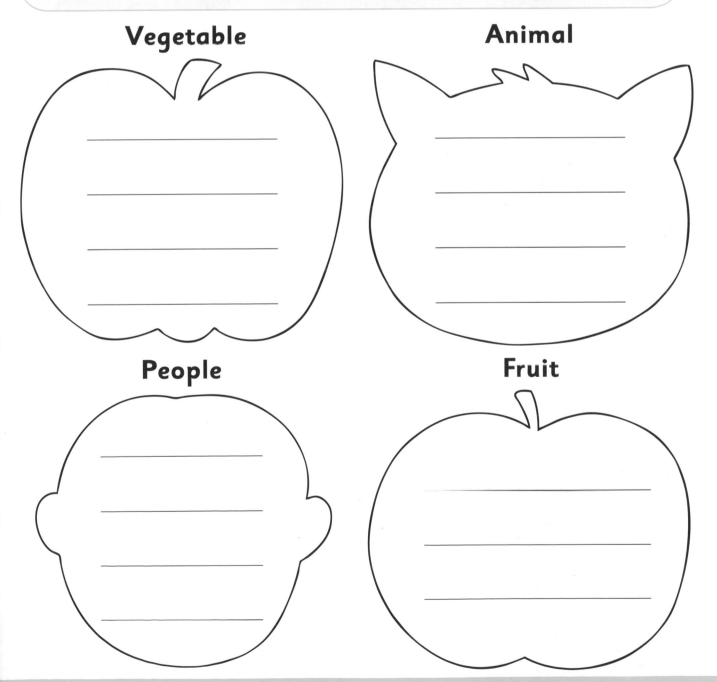

Vegetable

Animal

People

Fruit

How did you do?

At the beach

Choose the best naming word to complete the sentences below.

castle

book

crabs

cake

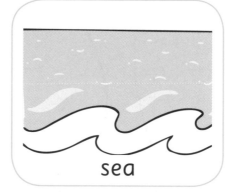
sea

sun

1. Amy went to swim in the _____.

2. The _____ was very hot.

3. The children built a fantastic _____ in the sand.

4. Mum lay on a sunbed, reading a _____.

5. Dad helped us find _____ near the rocks.

6. At lunchtime, we had sandwiches and _____.

How did you do?

Find the naming word

Underline the naming word in each sentence.

1. The house is old and spooky.

2. The train left early.

3. There was a bird flying high.

4. The blue river was very cold.

5. The girl ran away.

6. The duckling is small and fluffy.

7. A tall man shouted loudly.

Rewrite these sentences using a different naming word.

8. The television was boring.

_____

9. The garden was green and colourful.

_____

How did you do?

One or more?

> Plural means more than one.
> Singular means one.

Draw a line to join each word to the correct label.

cat

carpets

birds

spider

elephant

bananas

singular

plural

Write the plural for each of these words.

1. apple _____

2. chair _____

Write the singular for each of these words.

3. laptops _____

4. letters _____

How did you do?

Saying how many

Write the plural for each of these words.

1. brush _____

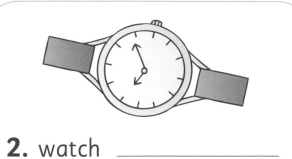

2. watch _____

3. glass _____

4. fox _____

Write the singular for each of these words.

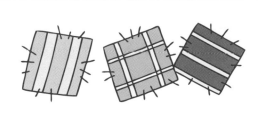

5. patches _____

6. hutches _____

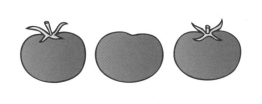

7. tomatoes _____

8. sixes _____

How did you do?

The right amount

Circle the best word for each of these sentences.

1. The **carpet / carpets** was dirty.

2. The **pizza / pizzas** were very hot.

3. The fairy godmother gave her three **wish / wishes**.

4. We opened some **box / boxes**.

5. They peeled the **potato / potatoes** for tea.

6. We waited for a long time and then two **bus / buses** came at once.

7. The **witch / witches** stirred up a spell in her cauldron.

8. The singer blew lots of **kiss / kisses** to her fans.

How did you do?

Is or are?

Singular → is
Plural → are

Fill in the missing words.

1. The boxes _____ empty.

2. The girl _____ going to school.

3. The boys _____ playing cricket.

4. The infant classes _____ going on a trip.

5. The dishes _____ in the cupboard.

6. This tomato _____ not ripe.

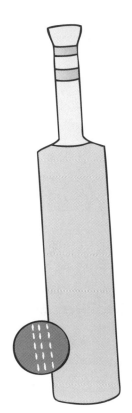

Change the bold words to plural and rewrite each sentence.

7. The **dress is** ready for the wedding.

_____

8. The **train is** late.

_____

How did you do?

Names of people and places

Rewrite each name so it starts with a capital letter.

	goldilocks	_____
	jack and jill	_____
	rapunzel	_____
	england	_____

Underline the names of people and places below.

Rewrite the sentences using a capital letter at the start of the names.

1. The beanstalk was hard for jack to climb.

_____

2. We went to paris for a holiday.

_____

How did you do?

Who? Where?

Answer the questions below.

1. What is your name?

_____

2. Where do you live?

_____

3. Where did you go on holiday?

_____

4. What is your teacher's name?

_____

5. What is your friend's name?

_____

Write a sentence using a place name.

_____

_____

How did you do?

Find it!

Underline names of people or places in these sentences.
Rewrite the sentences, putting capital letters in the right places.

1. My dog is called scamp.

_____

2. We had tea with uncle richard.

_____

3. We went to orlando for our holidays.

_____

4. Did you watch merlin cast a spell?

_____

5. Our head teacher is called mrs duncan.

_____

6. They walked until they got to weymouth.

_____

How did you do?

Who does it?

Add **er** to each word to make a new noun.

1. paint _____

2. clean _____

3. fight _____

4. work _____

Make new nouns by replacing the **e** at the end with **er**.

5. dance _____

6. bake _____

7. village _____

8. office _____

How did you do?

Find the ending

A suffix is a word ending.

Underline the suffix in these words.

1. enjoyment

4. happiness

2. motherhood

5. judgement

3. merriment

6. brotherhood

Decide which suffix could be added to each word. Write the new words in the correct spaces.

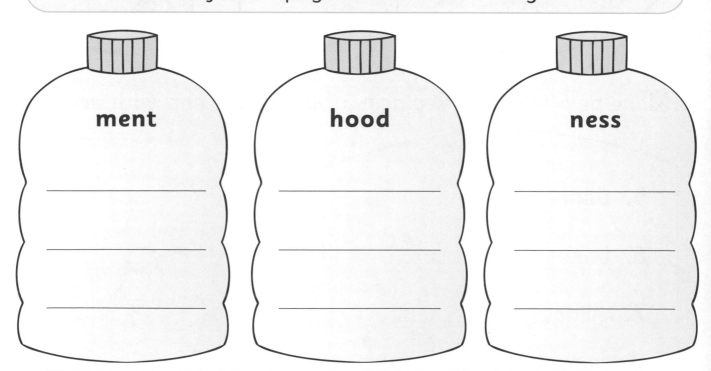

ill   refresh   pay   rude   kind   knight

ment

_____

_____

_____

hood

_____

_____

_____

ness

_____

_____

_____

Choose one of your new words and use it in a sentence.

_____

How did you do?

Which ending?

Circle the correct word for each of these sentences.

1. Alicia's **happihood / happiness / happiment** when she saw her bike was delightful.

2. Ahmed's **childhood / childness / childment** was full of games and fun.

3. The girl accepted her **punishhood / punishness / punishment**.

4. The **darkment / darkness / darkhood** of the forest was quite scary.

5. Their **neighbourment / neighbourhood / neighbourness** was very quiet.

6. The girl's **blindhood / blindment / blindness** did not stop her from running the race.

Write new words using each of these suffixes.

7. hood _____

8. ness _____

9. ment _____

How did you do?

Word sums

Make a new compound word from two smaller words.

Colour the two words the same colour. Use different colours for each new compound word.

Write your new compound words below.

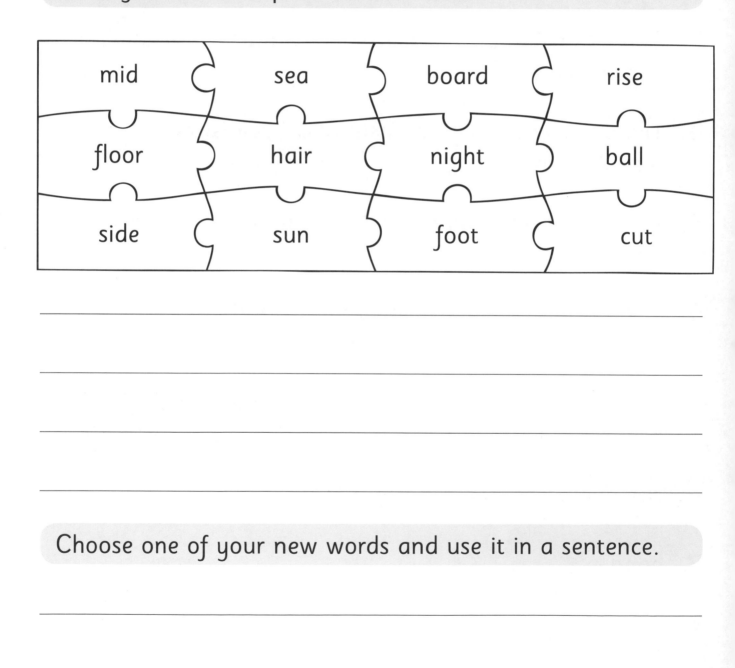

_____

_____

_____

_____

Choose one of your new words and use it in a sentence.

_____

_____

How did you do?

What is an adjective?

Adjectives are describing words.

Underline the adjectives in these phrases.

1. a rainy day

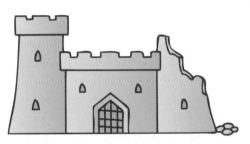

2. a mysterious present

3. a furry teddy

4. a ruined castle

5. a shiny mirror

6. a dark forest

7. a comfy chair

8. a fast car

How did you do?

Which adjective?

Choose the best adjective from the box to finish each sentence.

tall	messy	juicy	long	busy	warm

1. There was a _____ queue at the airport.

2. Oscar's bedroom was very _____.

3. We ate some _____ bread.

4. Jenny's tower was very _____.

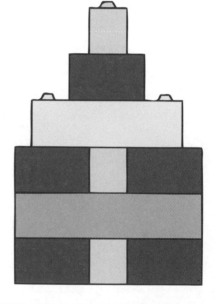

5. Omar liked the _____ apple.

6. The car park was very _____.

Choose one of the adjectives and write your own sentence.

_____

_____

How did you do?

Tell me more!

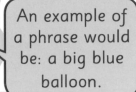

An example of a phrase would be: a big blue balloon.

Think of two adjectives to describe each of these pictures.

Then write a phrase to describe the picture using both the adjectives.

Adjective 1: _____

Adjective 2: _____

Phrase: _____

_____

Adjective 1: _____

Adjective 2: _____

Phrase: _____

_____

Adjective 1: _____

Adjective 2: _____

Phrase: _____

_____

Adjective 1: _____

Adjective 2: _____

Phrase: _____

_____

How did you do?

Colours

Colour the circles. Then use those colours to colour the picture.

Names of colours are adjectives.

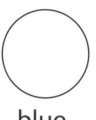 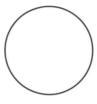 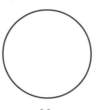 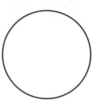

blue   green   yellow   red

Complete these sentences about the picture.

1. The _____ kite is flying in the sky.

2. Harry's hair is _____.

3. Olivia kicked the _____ ball.

How did you do?

Droogal the dragon

This is the beginning of a story. Make it better by adding some interesting adjectives. Use the words to help you.

Droogal was a _____ dragon. He lived in

a _____ castle. He had _____ teeth,

_____ eyes and _____ claws.

pointed   spiky   blobby   friendly   soppy
blue   terrible   pretty   powerful   perfect

One day Droogal saw a _____ boy

coming to his castle. The boy had _____

arms, _____ legs and _____ eyes.

He had a _____ dog.

tiny   massive   weak   flashing   crazy
gentle   skinny   funny   fierce   kind

How did you do?

Scary adventure

Finish the story by adding some really interesting adjectives.

I was woken by a _____ noise. I got up and saw a

_____ light. It led me up the _____ stairs. I

was in a _____ tower.

All I could see was a _____ _____ witch.

A _____ cauldron was bubbling on the fire.

_____ _____ smoke swirled up from it.

Write some more sentences to finish the adventure.
You must use one or two adjectives in each sentence.

_____

_____

_____

_____

How did you do?

Opposites

Rewrite these words so they start with **un**.

We can add **un** to the start of a word to change its meaning.

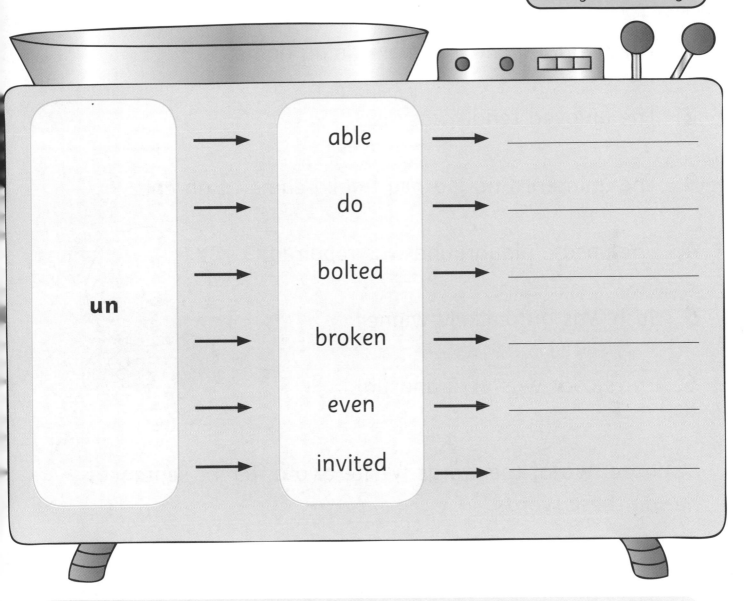

un		able	→	_____
	→	do	→	_____
	→	bolted	→	_____
	→	broken	→	_____
	→	even	→	_____
	→	invited	→	_____

Use two of your new words in a sentence.

_____

_____

How did you do?

Find un words

Underline the words that start with **un**.

1. The unhappy children were going home.

2. The unloved teddy was lost.

3. The uninteresting journey finally came to an end.

4. The unsafe playground was repaired.

5. Josh was an unlikely winner.

6. Erin's coat was very unusual.

Choose two of the words. Write two different sentences using these words.

7. _____

_____

8. _____

_____

How did you do?

Magic suffixes

We can make adjectives by adding the suffixes **less** and **ful**.
Words ending in **y** change **y** to **i** before adding the suffix.

Use the suffixes below to make two different adjectives from each of these words.

	ful	**less**
1. hope	_____	_____
2. use	_____	_____
3. care	_____	_____
4. mercy	_____	_____
5. help	_____	_____

Choose one pair of words from above. Write a sentence using each one. How has the suffix changed the meaning of these words?

6. _____

7. _____

How did you do?

Just add y

Add **y** to these words to make them into adjectives.

1. cloud _____   **3.** storm _____

2. rain _____   **4.** health _____

Turn these words into adjectives.

For words with a short vowel sound in the middle, double the last letter and add **y** to the end. For example: r**un** → run**ny**

5. sun _____   **7.** fun _____

6. fog _____   **8.** flop _____

Try turning these words into adjectives.

For words ending in **e**, change **e** to **y**. For example: shin**e** → shin**y**

9. ice _____   **11.** smoke _____

10. stone _____   **12.** taste _____

How did you do?

Adding er and est

Add **er** and **est** to these words to make new adjectives.

1. strong _____ _____

2. weak _____ _____

3. high _____ _____

Turn these words into adjectives.

4. wide _____ _____

5. strange _____ _____

6. rude _____ _____

For words ending in **e**, change **e** to **er** or **est**.

Try turning these words into adjectives.

7. happy _____ _____

8. funny _____ _____

9. snowy _____ _____

For words ending in **y**, change **y** to **i** and then add **er** or **est**.

How did you do?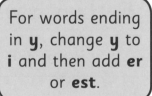

Bigger than?

These sentences do not make sense.

Underline the adjective in each one.

Then rewrite it by adding **er** or **est**, so that it makes sense.

1. My dog is friendly than John's.

_____

2. This carpet is the clean in the house.

_____

3. The film was scary than the one last week.

_____

4. Today is the cold day of the week.

_____

5. Lunch was healthy than breakfast.

_____

6. The river is at its wide here.

_____

How did you do?

Comparing

Use these adjectives in your own sentences.

1. grumpiest

_____

2. easier

_____

3. fastest

_____

4. sadder

_____

Underline the best adjective to use in each sentence.

5. The concert was the **louder / loudest** I have ever been to.

6. Jane was **lazier / laziest** than her older sister.

7. The kitten was the **cuter / cutest** of the litter.

How did you do?

Making adverbs

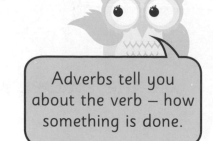

Add **ly** to these adjectives to make them into adverbs.

Adverbs tell you about the verb – how something is done.

1. sad _____

3. quick _____

2. slow _____

4. loud _____

Turn these words into adverbs.

5. creepy _____

For words ending in **y**, change **y** to **i** and then add **ly**.

6. angry _____

7. greedy _____

8. hasty _____

Choose two of the adverbs you made and use them each in a sentence.

9. _____

_____

10. _____

_____

How did you do?

How did I do it?

Write two adverbs that could describe each action below.

Which verb?

Underline the adverb in the sentences below.

1. The snail went slowly up the path.

2. The girl jogged quickly around the track.

3. Ranvir tiptoed carefully downstairs.

Write the adverb and the verb it describes in the table.

	adverb	verb it describes
1.		
2.		
3.		

Rewrite these sentences using a different adverb.

4. Erin smiled sweetly at her mum.

_____

5. Jack shouted angrily at his friend.

_____

How did you do?

What are you doing?

Circle each doing word.

1. I read a book.

2. I climb a tree.

3. I eat a pizza.

4. I sit on a chair.

5. I ride a bike.

6. I play football.

7. I walk in the rain.

8. I sweep the floor.

How did you do?

Using doing words

Choose the right doing word from the box to complete each sentence below.

cooking   sleeping   planting   cutting
running   reading   walking   swimming

1. Josh is _____ a seed.

2. Grandpa is _____ in bed.

3. The dog is _____ for his ball.

4. Dad is _____ dinner.

5. Mum is _____ the grass.

6. I am _____ a story.

7. Sophie is _____ in the sea.

8. We are _____ to school.

How did you do?

Unzip it!

Use **un** to change these verbs.

1. zip _____   4. peg _____

2. load _____   5. pick _____

3. mask _____   6. plug _____

Use each of these words in a sentence.

7. zip

_____

8. unzip

_____

9. plug

_____

10. unplug

_____

Untangle the sentences

Choose the best word from the box for each sentence below.

> unplugged   unrolled   untangle
> unpinned   undo

1. We _____ our sleeping bags in the tent.

2. It took ages to _____ the balls of wool.

3. Dad _____ all our electric appliances when we went on holiday.

4. The dressmaker _____ the hem.

5. She could not _____ her zip – it was stuck!

Write the above words without **un** at the beginning.

_____   _____   _____

_____   _____

How did you do?

Action time!

Add **s** or **es** to the doing words in brackets to make each sentence correct.

1. He _____ football.
(play)

2. She _____ her hair.
(brush)

3. He _____ a book.
(read)

4. She _____ her teddy.
(kiss)

5. He _____ his hands.
(wash)

6. She _____ fast.
(run)

7. He _____ some paint.
(mix)

8. She _____ a toy.
(fix)

How did you do?

Which doing word?

Circle the correct doing word to finish each sentence.

1. I **go / goes** to school.

2. Jack **walk / walks** in the park.

3. Amy **like / likes** apples.

4. Ranvir **build / builds** a tower.

5. We **paint / paints** a big picture.

6. They **live / lives** in this house.

7. Dad **clean / cleans** the kitchen.

8. Gran **drive / drives** her car.

How did you do?

Taking care of a kitten

Write instructions to help someone take care of a kitten.

Write in complete sentences.

Use the present tense.

The present tense means it's happening now.

food   water   bed   sleep   vet

injections   healthy   disease

1. _____

_____

2. _____

_____

3. _____

_____

4. _____

_____

How did you do?

Wanted!

Write a description of this villain.

Include details that will help people catch him.

Use the present tense.

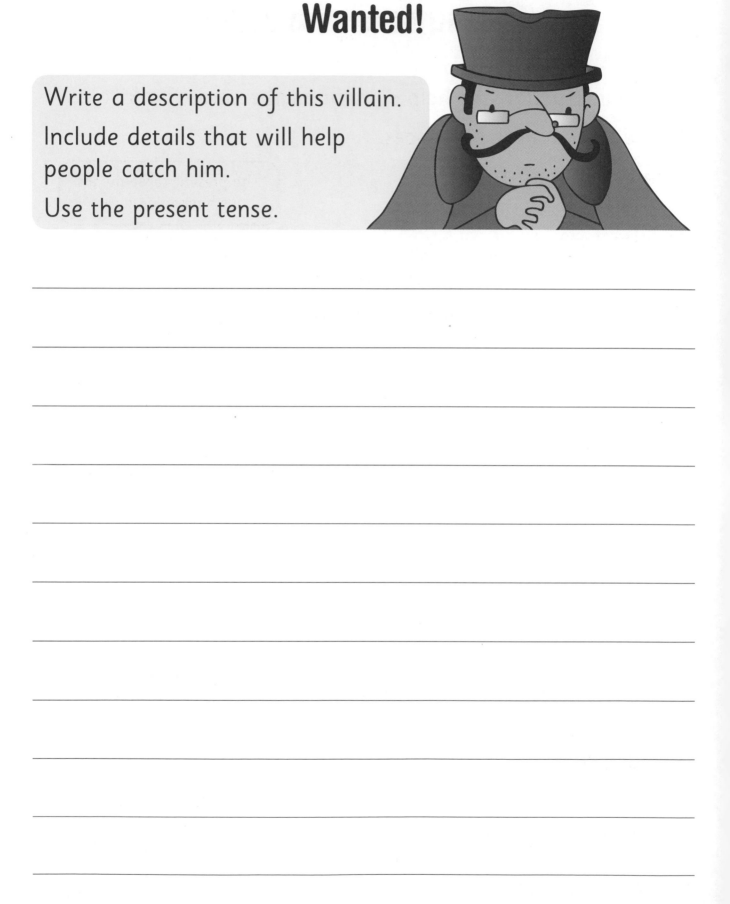

How did you do?

Adding ed

Change these verbs to the past tense by adding **ed**.

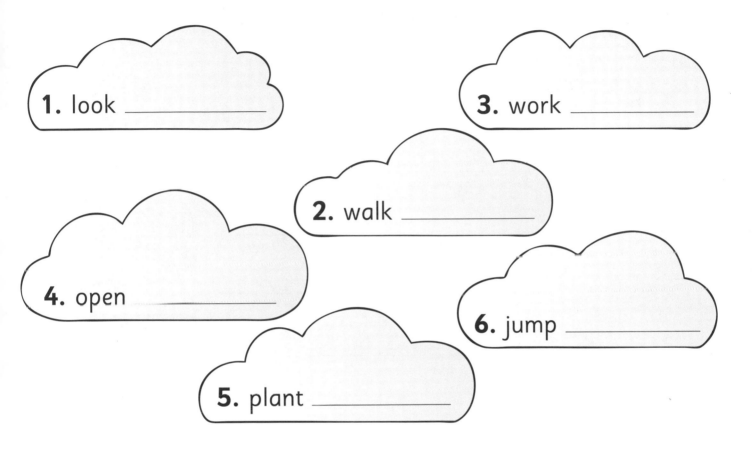

1. look _____

3. work _____

2. walk _____

4. open _____

6. jump _____

5. plant _____

Underline the verbs in these sentences.

7. Josh cooked spaghetti for tea.

8. Liz mixed some pancakes.

9. Esme walked the dog.

10. Ben planted a tree.

How did you do?

What have they done?

Change each verb to the past tense.

Use it to write a sentence about each picture.

1. bang: _____

_____

2. whisper: _____

_____

3. search: _____

_____

4. laugh: _____

_____

5. listen: _____

_____

6. dust: _____

_____

How did you do?

What happens next?

Read these story beginnings. Write what happens next.
Use the past tense.

The waves crashed and broke against the rocks.
As the tide crept up higher, Adam wondered
how he could possibly escape. Suddenly he
saw a faint glow of light in the distance...

_____

_____

_____

The train juddered and jerked and came to a
sharp stop. Sarah looked outside into the
darkness. All she could see were some strange
creatures coming towards the train.
Who were they? What did they want?

_____

_____

_____

How did you do?

45

Changing tenses

Write sentences using each verb below.
Write one sentence in the present tense.
Write one sentence in the past tense.

1. have: Today I _____

Yesterday I _____

2. say: Today he _____

Yesterday he _____

3. make: Today they _____

Yesterday they _____

4. swim: Today Asha _____

Yesterday Asha _____

5. sleep: Today Sam _____

Yesterday Sam _____

How did you do?

Time machine

Oh dear! This story is being sucked into a time machine so everything will have happened in the past.

Underline the verbs in this story.

Rewrite the story in the past tense.

The goat wants to eat the grass on the other side of the bridge. It is much greener there. He begins to cross the rickety bridge. As he goes across, an angry voice growls, "Who is that trip trapping across my bridge?"
The goat says, "It is only me, the smallest billy goat."

_____

_____

_____

_____

_____

How did you do?

Am, are or is?

am, are and is are helper verbs.

Choose the best helper verb to go in these sentences.

1. I _____ looking at a computer.

2. He _____ swimming in the pool.

3. Mum and Dad _____ making dinner.

4. Richard _____ working hard.

5. Emily _____ watching a play.

6. The rabbits _____ playing in the sunlight.

Tick the correct words in the sentence below.

The six sentences above describe things that:

☐ are happening all the time.

☐ are happening now.

☐ happened in the past.

How did you do?

Holidays

Use helper verbs to rewrite these sentences so they describe something that is happening now.

is   am   are

1. We pack our case.

_____

2. I get in a taxi.

_____

3. We go to the airport.

_____

4. We fly on a plane.

_____

5. He lands on a sunny island.

_____

How did you do?

What is happening?

Use the helper verbs: **am**, **is**, **are**

Write a sentence about each picture to describe what is happening.

1. _____

_____

2. _____

_____

3. _____

_____

4. _____

_____

5. _____

_____

6. _____

_____

How did you do?

Country watch

Use the helper verbs:
was, **were**

Use the helper verbs to write about what each animal was doing yesterday.

1. _____

_____

2. _____

_____

3. _____

_____

4. _____

_____

5. _____

_____

How did you do?

In the mud

Write one sentence below each picture. Make sure you use a capital letter and full stop.

i went to the park
she went in the mud

my dog went too
dad was cross

How did you do?

New shoes

Colour each capital letter. Underline each full stop. Then count the sentences.

Raj went out with Mum. He got some new shoes. Then he went to see his gran. He showed her his new shoes. She liked them.

There are _____ sentences.

It was very cold. Sally and Josh went out. They played in Sally's garden. Then they went to Josh's house. His dad made them hot chocolate. They sat by the fire. Soon they were warm.

There are _____ sentences.

Sam can't swim. He goes to lessons. He likes to play in the water. His little sister can swim. His big brother can swim. Sam doesn't like swimming.

There are _____ sentences.

How did you do?

53

Peter's monster

Find seven sentences in this story. Change any letters that should be capitals and add the full stops.

Peter made a monster it was bigger than he was

Peter gave his monster a hat he gave it a coat he

gave it glasses he put the monster in a chair it gave

the teacher a fright

Write two sentences about something you have made.

_____

_____

_____

How did you do?

Mind the gap

Choose a word for each space.

It _____ cold.

| put | is | we |

_____ on your hat.

| Snow | Then | Put |

Then _____ can go.

| your | look | we |

I _____ something to eat.

| want | hungry | you |

Do _____ want an apple?

| am | eat | you |

How did you do?

My brother

Write the best word from the bottom of the page in each gap.

1. My _____ will be ten in _____ .

2. Where did _____ get _____ hat?

3. _____ has got a _____ bike.

4. _____ you seen my red _____?

5. _____ you help _____ open this box?

6. We were _____ home last _____ .

March   He   brother

at   night   me   hat

new   Can   you

that   Have

How did you do?

Signs

Use each group of words to write a sentence.

Write a sentence for the last picture.

Make sure each sentence makes sense.

Draw pictures to go with the first two sentences.

run. do not Please

the away. Put brushes

our to school. Welcome

How did you do?

Using 'and'

Use **and** to join these sentences.
Make sure there is no repetition.

1. I am hungry. I want to eat.

_____

2. I am tired. I need to go to bed.

_____

3. Craig likes football. Craig likes cricket.

_____

4. We are in Class 2. My brother is in Class 4.

_____

5. Dogs eat meat. Dogs like long walks.

_____

6. Birds build nests. Birds lay eggs.

_____

How did you do?

Using 'but'

Match each beginning with an ending.

Beginning

The sun was shining
The dog was barking
The car stopped
The bread was stale
We wanted more fish

Ending

it wasn't old.
the pet shop didn't have any.
it was getting cloudy.
there was no one there.
there was plenty of petrol.

Write the full sentence, joining each part using **but**.

_____

_____

_____

_____

_____

How did you do?

Joining words

Colour the best joining word for each sentence.
Cross out any words, full stops or capital letters that you don't need.

1. It's getting late. (and) (but) I want to go home.

2. Tom opened the back door. (and) (but) The snow blew inside.

3. I want to buy a drink. (and) (but) I haven't got any money.

4. I want to go outside. (and) (but) I want to play on the trampoline.

5. Amy was scared of the dog. (and) (but) It was friendly.

6. I want a gerbil for Christmas. (and) (but) I want a cage.

How did you do?

What comes next?

Write an ending for each sentence.
The joining word in each sentence may help you.

1. I like carrots but _____

_____

2. Malala opened the door and _____

_____

3. Amelia wanted a hamster but _____

_____

4. The plant was dry and _____

_____

5. I wrote a story but _____

_____

6. We went camping but _____

_____

How did you do?

Getting to know you

Make each group of words into a question.

Write them in the speech bubbles below.

Write your own question in the last speech bubble.

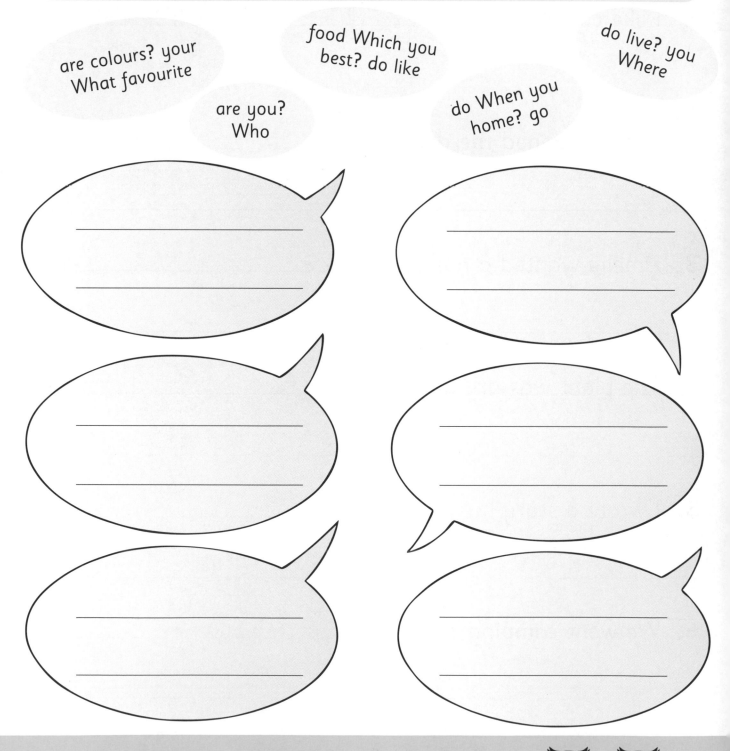

How did you do?

Choosing question words

Choose the best question word from the box for each sentence.

Who   Which   Where   When   What   Why

1. _____ is the toothpaste?

2. _____ are we going to Gran and Grandad's?

3. _____ way are we going?

4. _____ has taken my toy?

5. _____ are we stopping here?

6. _____ are you doing?

Choose a question word and write your own question.

_____

_____

How did you do?

What is the question?

Here are answers to questions.

Write the question for each answer, using the question words from the box to help you.

Who   Which   Where   When   What   Why

1. I have a dog and a cat.

_____

2. I am going to Greece for my holiday.

_____

3. My teacher is Miss Brown.

_____

4. I am going to the cinema on Friday.

_____

5. I am making a cake because it is my mum's birthday.

_____

How did you do?

All about dinosaurs

What would you like to know about dinosaurs?
Ask four questions.

1. When _____

_____

2. Where _____

_____

3. Why _____

_____

4. What _____

_____

How did you do?

Excuses

Make up excuses to finish the sentences below.
It doesn't matter if your excuses are silly!

1. I didn't do my homework because _____

_____

2. I didn't eat my dinner because _____

_____

3. I didn't dry the dishes because _____

_____

4. I didn't clean the hamster out because _____

_____

5. I didn't go to the jungle because _____

_____

6. I didn't fly on the magic carpet because _____

_____

How did you do?

Which way?

An explorer is trying to choose the best way to find treasure.

Choose pairs of routes below and use **and** to join them. One has been done for you.

over the mountains

through the jungle

across the river

through the swamp

over the cliffs

over the rapids

1. Through the jungle and over the rapids.

2. _____

3. _____

4. _____

5. _____

6. _____

7. _____

8. _____

How did you do?   ✔   ?

Which joining word?

Choose the best joining word for these sentences.

and   or   but

1. It is snowing _____ the buses have stopped running.

2. You can ride a bike _____ you can't go on the road.

3. Do you want to eat pizza _____ spaghetti?

4. I like getting up early _____ watching cartoons.

Finish these sentences.

5. Asha did not want to go into the dark woods or

_____

6. Misha peered through the gloomy glass but

_____

7. Carefully, Andrew climbed through into the hole and

_____

How did you do?

Find the join

Underline the joining word in each sentence.

1. We can go for a walk when we have tidied up.

2. You can play in the garden if it stops raining.

3. Oliver likes doing jigsaws and playing with his train.

4. Sophie is painting the doors red because it is her favourite colour.

5. Dad was worried that we were going to be late.

6. Mum said we could have mango or apple juice.

List the joining words you have found.

_____   _____   _____

_____   _____   _____

Choose two joining words and write you own sentences.

7. _____

8. _____

How did you do?

Trains

When, **if**, **that**, and **because** are all joining words.

Choose the best joining word for these sentences.

| when | if | that | because |

1. The train from Blackpool will arrive _____ the London train has departed.

2. The train to Glasgow is late _____ there are leaves on the line.

3. You might find a seat _____ lots of people get off the train.

4. The ticket inspector checked _____ everyone had a ticket.

Use each joining word in your own sentences.

5. _____.

6. _____.

7. _____.

8. _____.

How did you do?

Beginnings and endings

Look at the sentence beginnings and endings below.

Beginning	Ending
I would like to be a fireman	I am older.
We put balloons up	it was Mum's birthday.
We planted sunflower seeds	will grow in summer.
We could go to the zoo	go to the theme park.
They were going to buy some fruit	they went to the supermarket.

Write each sentence using the best joining word to link each part.

when   if   that   because   or

_____

_____

_____

_____

_____

How did you do?

Types of sentence

What type of sentence is each person saying?
Draw lines to match the sentences to the correct type.

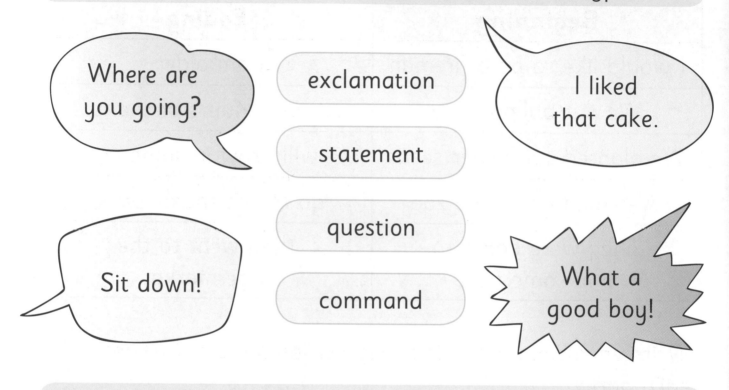

Write your own sentence in the empty speech bubble.
Join it to the correct label.

exclamation   statement   question   command

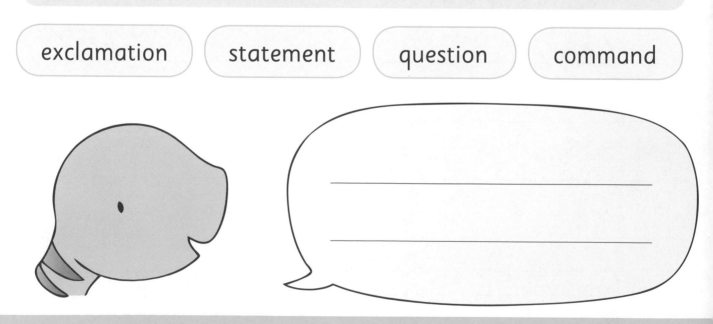

How did you do?

Scamp

Write in the best punctuation mark for each sentence.

Write your own sentence about Scamp.
Choose the best punctuation to end your sentence.

_____

_____

How did you do?

What are they saying?

Write a sentence to match each picture.
Use each punctuation mark (**.** **?** and **!**).

Draw your own picture. Write a question to match it. Use the correct punctuation at the end.

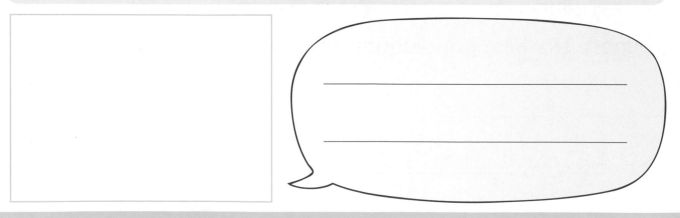

How did you do?

Describing animals

An adjective and a noun make a noun phrase.

Use the adjectives for each animal to write your own noun phrases.

fierce   fast

powerful   wild

_____ crocodile

_____ crocodile

_____, _____ crocodile

_____ snake

_____ snake

_____, _____ snake

curly   slithery

dry   long

cute   furry

cuddly   tabby

_____ kitten

_____ kitten

_____, _____ kitten

How did you do?

Finding noun phrases

An example of a noun phrase is: the pink ball.

Underline the noun phrases in these sentences.

1. I enjoyed reading the exciting story.

2. The black car swerved to avoid us.

3. I drew a circle using a sharp pencil.

4. I took the steaming buns out of the oven.

5. I fell asleep in the soft comfortable bed.

6. The tiny grey mouse ran under the cupboard.

Choose two of the sentences above.
Rewrite them using different noun phrases.

7. _____

_____

8. _____

_____

How did you do?

Giant

You can use more than one adjective to describe a noun.

Use the picture and adjectives to help you write a description of this giant.
Remember to use noun phrases.

huge terrifying knobbly hairy
enormous loud sharp thick
bulging long rough pointed
fat spotty tall scary wide
dangerous noisy

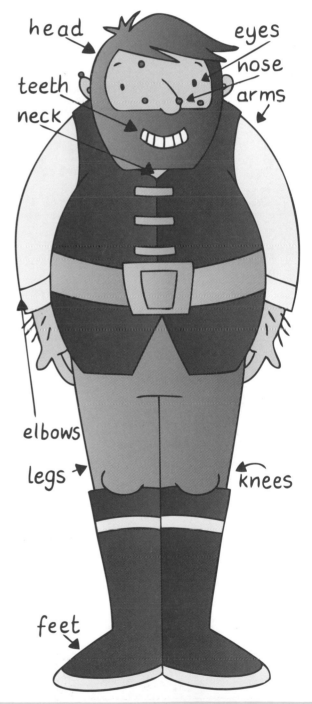

head   eyes
nose
teeth   arms
neck

elbows
legs   knees

feet

_____

_____

_____

_____

_____

_____

_____

How did you do?

Capital letters and full stops

Rewrite these sentences, starting with a capital letter and ending with a full stop.

1. i like apples

_____

2. jane is going to school

_____

3. we are eating tea

_____

4. the dog wants a walk

_____

5. i am playing in the garden

_____

6. he has a big bedroom

_____

How did you do?

Is it a question?

Decide if these sentences are questions or statements.
Add a full stop or a question mark to the end.

1. Are you going to the party ( )

2. It is Monday ( )

3. We need to go shopping ( )

4. Have you made lunch ( )

5. Where is my book ( )

6. It is on the table ( )

How did you do?

Cars

Write the missing punctuation in the boxes.

. ! ?

1. Is it a red car ☐

2. What a red car ☐

3. Get the red car ☐

4. It is a red car ☐

5. The car is quite fast ☐

6. Wow, that's fast ☐

7. Why is it fast ☐

8. Make it faster ☐

How did you do?

What's wrong?

Rewrite the sentences. Remember to add in the missing capital letters. Then add the missing **? !** or **.**

1. i am sitting on a chair

_____

2. are we winning

_____

3. what a beautiful day

_____

4. come here

_____

5. where is the cat

_____

6. it is snowing

_____

How did you do?

Punctuate me!

Add the missing capital letters and punctuation to these sentences. The first one has been done for you.

1. J̶ames was going on holiday.

2. he was going on a train to the seaside

3. he ate some crisps

4. ouch a crisp got stuck in his teeth

5. what a long way

6. when will we get there

Now write two more sentences about their trip to the seaside. Use capital letters and correct punctuation.

_____

_____

_____

How did you do?

Adverts

Add the missing capital letters and punctuation to these adverts.

Creamy choc-chews

need a taste sensation
buy creamy choc-chews

choc-chews

the best-ever chocolate bar

Thrill-seeker climbing frame

want an adventure
our climbing frame gives
exercise and thrills

buy it now

Grammar and Punctuation Workbooks

GRAMMAR + PUNCTUATION

do you find grammar tricky

have you had punctuation nightmares

you need our workbooks

the answer to your problems

How did you do?

Names of people and places

Rewrite these words, using a capital letter to start the names of people and places.

london

amy

fluffy

scotland

tom

blackpool

Rewrite these sentences, using a capital letter to start the names of people and places.

1. We enjoyed going to scarborough.

2. My gran went to wales on a coach.

3. I love walking rover, my dog.

How did you do?

My favourite day

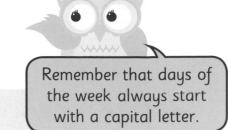

Remember that days of the week always start with a capital letter.

Complete the sentences.

> Monday   Tuesday   Wednesday
> Thursday   Friday   Saturday   Sunday

On _____ we _____

On _____ we _____

On _____ we _____

On _____ we _____

On _____ we _____

On _____ and _____ we don't
go to school.

My favourite day of the week is _____ because

_____

_____

_____

_____

How did you do?

Capital letters

Rewrite these sentences. Add the missing capital letters.

1. Our head teacher is mr thomas.

_____

2. Jack and i went to preston last week.

_____

3. My cat is called pippi.

_____

4. Our favourite place is the lake district.

_____

5. Are you going to auntie rachel's?

_____

6. I got a letter from edinburgh.

_____

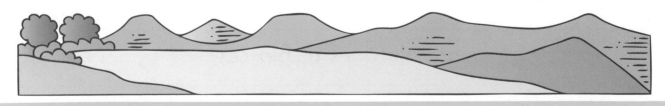

How did you do?

Find the comma

Circle each comma in these sentences.

1. My friends are Jason, Amelia, Ranvir and Ahmed.

2. Spring is in March, April, May and part of June.

3. France, Spain, Germany, Belgium and Holland
are all in Europe.

4. Red, white and blue are the
colours of the Union Jack flag.

Finish these sentences and circle each comma.

5. For breakfast I eat _____, _____,
_____ and _____.

6. I have been to _____, _____,
_____ and _____.

7. _____, _____, _____ and
_____ are all types of big cat.

How did you do?

Missing commas

Add in the missing commas in each of these sentences.

1. I am going to the newsagent the post office the bakers and the library.

2. I like to play football cricket basketball and rounders.

3. My favourite colours are blue indigo purple and green.

4. The world is split into the continents of Asia Africa Australia Antarctica Europe North America and South America.

5. London has many famous landmarks including Big Ben Buckingham Palace the London Eye and Westminster Abbey.

6. Daniel's school is made up of Nursery Reception Key Stage 1 and Key Stage 2.

7. We can travel to town by bike bus train or tram.

8. We have roses sunflowers begonias and dahlias in our garden.

How did you do?

List it!

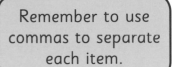

Remember to use commas to separate each item.

Use the lists below to finish these sentences.

Use four items in each list.

fish	vegetables	furniture	in your classroom
cod	potatoes	chairs	desks
pike	cauliflower	tables	whiteboard
plaice	broccoli	beds	cupboards
halibut	carrots	sofas	displays
sole	leeks	televisions	paints

1. There are lots of fish including _____

_____

2. Some of the vegetables we eat are _____

_____

3. At home we have furniture such as _____

_____

4. In our classroom we have _____

_____

How did you do?

Match the words

Match the words to the correct word with an apostrophe.

it is

its'
it's
i'ts

did not

did'nt
di'dnt
didn't

they are

they're
theyr'e
the'yre

could not

couldnt'
could'nt
couldn't

we have

we've
wev'e
w'eve

cannot

can't
c'ant
ca'nt

you will

youl'l
youll'
you'll

How did you do?

What am I?

Look at each word joined with an apostrophe in the sentences below.

Write the two words it stands for. The first one has been done for you.

1. It's raining.

____It is____

2. I'd love to come to your party.

_____

3. We've been to the cinema.

_____

4. I can't believe it!

_____

5. I wouldn't go into that dark cave.

_____

6. That's not a monster!

_____

7. They didn't arrive until very late.

_____

8. We'll go down to the beach after lunch.

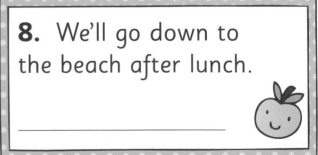

_____

How did you do?

Apostrophes for missing letters

Rewrite these words using an apostrophe to shorten them.

1. have not _____

2. did not _____

3. cannot _____

4. would not _____

5. I have _____

6. we have _____

7. I am _____

8. she is _____

Rewrite the words in **bold**, using an apostrophe to shorten them.

9. **I will** go to the match.

_____

10. **They have** given us a present.

_____

11. We **could not** find the right way.

_____

12. She **has not** read that book yet.

_____

How did you do?

Whose is it?

Mum   Dad   Oliver   Ibrahim   Shima   Grandad

flowers   football   book   laptop   cake   apple

Choose a person.

Choose an object for that person.

Write who the object belongs to.

Remember to use an apostrophe.

Example: Grandad's flowers

_____   _____

_____   _____

_____   _____

Write a sentence using one of the phrases above.

_____

How did you do?

Find the owner

Find the apostrophes in these sentences.

Underline the owner and the thing they own.

Write who the thing belongs to. The first one has been started for you.

1. <u>Ethan's bathtime</u> was lots of fun.

The bathtime belongs to _____ .

2. Sam's scooter was very fast.

The _____ belongs to _____ .

3. The butterfly's wings were beautiful.

The _____ belong to the _____ .

4. The coach's journey took them on a motorway.

The _____ belongs to the _____ .

5. The class's trip was to be on Monday.

The _____ belongs to the _____ .

6. This autumn's weather was very warm.

The _____ belongs to the _____ .

How did you do?

Missing apostrophes

Add the missing apostrophes into these sentences.

1. I found Dads wallet.

2. We are going to Ellies party.

3. They climbed up the aircrafts steps.

4. That is Jamess basketball.

5. It is our schools concert.

6. The cats whiskers help her find things in the dark.

7. We stayed out of the suns heat.

8. There was a lot of noise from the buss engine.

How did you do?

Well done!

Cut-out your reward Ollie.

Name:

....

You have completed

Grammar and punctuation

For ages 5–7

Age: ....

Date: ....